NEW HORIZONS IN ENGLISH 2

SECOND EDITION

LARS MELLGREN
MICHAEL WALKER

Consulting Editor:
JOHN A. UPSHUR
English Language Institute
University of Michigan

Shih-Kan King.

⚛ **ADDISON-WESLEY PUBLISHING COMPANY**

Reading, Massachusetts · Menlo Park, California · Don Mills, Ontario
Amsterdam · London · Manila · Singapore · Sydney · Tokyo

A publication of the World Language Division

Illustrations by Akihito Shirakawa

Photographs: p. 8, Elihu Blotnick; p. 53, Rafael Millán; p. 85, Swiss National Tourist Office; p. 88, The Perkins School For The Blind; p. 90, NASA; p. 100, G. Robert McConnell; p. 103, Rafael Millán.

ISBN 0-201-05059-5
  CDEFGHIJKLM-VH-898765

INTRODUCTION

NEW HORIZONS IN ENGLISH is a communication-centered, six-level, basal series planned and written to make the learning of English as a second language effective and rewarding. Stimulating opportunities to practice listening, speaking, reading, and writing skills develop independence and confidence in the use of English. Thoughtfully chosen vocabulary gives students the words they need to communicate in their new language in a variety of situations; carefully paced introduction of grammatical and structural concepts helps insure a strong foundation of communication skills.

Important to every learner is a sense of achievement, a feeling that he or she has successfully accomplished the tasks presented. Motivation, the desire to learn, is equally important. NEW HORIZONS IN ENGLISH is written to satisfy both needs: to provoke, through selection of topics, vocabulary, and illustrations, a genuine interest in learning more, and to pace and schedule material in such a way that achievement and mastery are facilitated. The content moves in systematic small steps, never overwhelming the learner, and each step is reinforced from unit to unit and level to level, in combination with new material. The progression of learning is planned, sequential, and cumulative. There is minimum potential for error and maximum potential for easy, satisfying mastery.

The language used in NEW HORIZONS IN ENGLISH is contemporary and relevant. Most important, it is English that students can and will use outside the classroom. Natural exchanges and dialogues arise from the real-life situations that form unit themes. Readings and written exercises are related to these themes, rounding out each unit. A strong listening strand, running throughout the series, builds student ability to derive meaning, both explicit and implicit, from spoken material. The emphasis on speaking and listening, with meaning always paramount, means that oral communicative competence develops early and is broadened and deepened as students move through the series. Parallel development of reading and writing skills promotes competence in other communication areas at the same time.

Dialogues and readings from the texts, and many of the exercises, are recorded on the optional tape cassette program, which provides models of American pronunciation and intonation. Separate pronunciation exercises in the first and second books help students associate particular consonant and vowel sounds (always in the context of words) with their English spellings.

Each level of NEW HORIZONS IN ENGLISH includes a workbook to provide additional practice and application of skills and vocabulary introduced in the text. A series of picture cards, the NEW HORIZONS IN ENGLISH PICTURE SHOW, may be used to help present vocabulary and generate conversation. An associated series, *Skill Sharpeners 1-4*, includes a variety of exercises and activities that further reinforce and extend the skills and concepts taught in NEW HORIZONS IN ENGLISH.

A complete program to build communicative competence, NEW HORIZONS IN ENGLISH provides motivation, mastery, and a sense of achievement. Every student—and every teacher—needs the feeling of pride in a job well done. NEW HORIZONS IN ENGLISH, with its unbeatable formula for classroom success, insures that this need will be filled.

CONTENTS

NEW HORIZONS IN ENGLISH 2

SECOND EDITION

—Dad, can I go downtown?
—Why? What do you want to do?
—I want to go to the movies.
—When do you want to go?
—Now.
—How do you want to go?
—By car—*your* car.
—Sorry. I want to use the car tonight.

Do you like to dance?	Yes, I do. No, I don't.

1. Do you like to swim? 5. Do you like to skate?

2. Do you like to read? 6. Do you like to ski?

3. Do you like to talk? 7. Do you like to study?

4. Do you like to type? 8. Do you like to paint?

Do you like apples?

Yes, I do. Do <u>you</u>?   Yes, I do too.
No, I don't.

No, I <u>don't</u>. Do <u>you</u>?   Yes, I do.
No, I don't either.

1. pineapples 2. coconuts 3. potatoes 4. beans 5. lettuce

6. chicken 7. lamb 8. pork 9. beef 10. fish

—Do you want to **play tennis**?

—Yes, I do.

—Do you have a **racket**?

—Of course.

—Well, let's go!

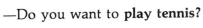

1. **play backgammon**
   backgammon board

2. **play football**
   football

3. **play soccer**
   ball

4. **play table tennis**
   paddle 球拍

5. **play the piano**
   music book

6. **sail** 帆船
   sailboat

What do you have in there?

I have a guitar.

---

1. What do you have in there?

I have a cat.

2. What do they have in there?

They have a dog.

3. What do you two have in there?

We have a drum.

4. What do you have in there?

I have a pineapple.

5. What do you have in there?

I have a soccer ball.

What do you want to play?		I want to play tennis.

1. What do you want to read?

I want to read comic books.

有趣

2. What do you want to eat?

I want to eat fish.

3. What do you want to drink?

I want to drink coffee.

4. What do you want to wear?

I want to wear jeans.

穿着　工作服牛仔

5. What do they want to paint?

They want to paint the house.

6. What do they want to play?

They want to play the drums.

7. What do you want to clean?

I want to clean the window.

—Don't you want to go to the **movies** with me?
—No, I don't.
—Well, where *do* you want to go?
—I want to go to the **theater**.

1. library   football stadium

2. concert   party

3. museum   disco

—How do you come to school?
—By **bus**.

1. train   2. school bus   3. scooter

4. bicycle   5. motorcycle   6. taxi

When do you want to play?  **In the morning.**

1. When do you want to swim?  In the afternoon.

2. When do you want to eat?  At noon.

3. When do you want to go to the movies? In the evening.

4. When do you want to watch TV? At night.

5. When do you want to go to sleep? At midnight.

My name is Joe Banks. I'm Canadian. I live in Toronto. I have one brother, Don. Don and my father have a service station. We all like cars. Don and my father work at the station every day. I work there on Saturday. I talk to the people and wash their windows. I give them gas, too. Don and I have an old car. We want to buy a new one this year.

1. What's the boy's name?
2. What's his nationality?
3. What do Don and his father have?
4. What do they all like?
5. When do Don and his father work at the station?
6. What can Joe do?
7. What do Don and Joe want to buy?

HOW ABOUT *YOU?*

1. What's your name?
2. What's your nationality?
3. Where do you live?
4. How many brothers and sisters do you have?
5. Do you work?
6. What do you do? What do you want to do?
7. Do you have a car?
8. Do you want to buy a new car?
9. What else do you want to buy this year?

LISTEN & UNDERSTAND

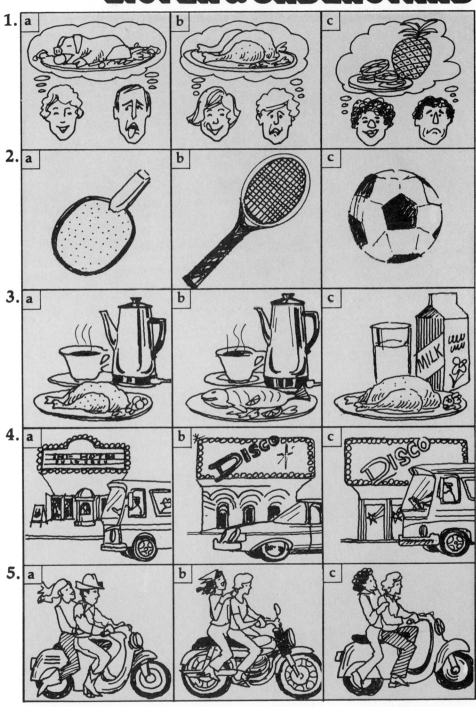

BASICS

| STATEMENTS: | I want to play tennis.
They have a guitar. |

| YES-NO QUESTIONS: | Do you want to play football?
Do you have a racket?
Do you like to dance?
Do you like apples? |

| INFORMATION QUESTIONS: | What do you want to do?
When do you want to play?
What do you have in there?
How do you come to school? |

| SHORT ANSWERS: | Yes, I do.
No, I don't. |

| CONTRACTION: | let us ⟶ let's |

VOCABULARY/EXPRESSIONS

backgammon board	lettuce	scooter
beef	live	service station
bicycle	motorcycle	talk
by	music book	use
chicken	paddle	want
coconuts	paint	why
disco	pineapple(s)	work
downtown	pork	
either	potatoes	go to sleep
football stadium	sail	in there
gas	sailboat	Let's go.
house	school	Of course.
lamb	school bus	

—What does your son do?
—He's a tennis player.
—My son is a truck driver.
—Does he like it?
—No, he doesn't.
—Why not?
—He doesn't like work!

Does he play football?  No, he doesn't.
Does he play tennis? Yes, he does.

1. Does he drive a taxi?  No, he doesn't.
   Does he drive a bus? Yes, he does.

2. Does he carry baggage?  No, he doesn't.
   Does he carry mail? Yes, he does.

3. Does she sing?  No, she doesn't.
   Does she teach? Yes, she does.

4. Does she play golf? No, she doesn't.
   Does she dance? Yes, she does.

5. Does she drive a taxi? 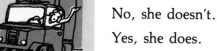 No, she doesn't.
   Does she drive a truck? Yes, she does.

6. Does he dance? 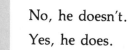 No, he doesn't.
   Does he cook? Yes, he does.

7. Does she clean windows? No, she doesn't.
   Does she sing? Yes, she does.

a tennis player   a taxi driver   a truck driver

a rider   a newspaper boy   a singer

a chef   a writer   a waiter

1. What does a tennis player do?   She plays tennis.

2. What does a taxi driver do?   He drives a taxi.

3. What does a truck driver do?   He drives a truck.

4. What does a rider do?   She rides horses.

5. What does a newspaper boy do?   He delivers newspapers.

6. What does a singer do?   She sings.

7. What does a chef do?   He cooks.

8. What does a writer do?   She writes.

9. What does a waiter do?   He waits on tables.

What's this woman?
What does she do?

She's a bus driver.
She drives a bus.

1. What's this woman?
   What does she do?

   She's a tennis player.
   She plays tennis.

2. What's this man?
   What does he do?

   He's a chef.
   He cooks.

3. What's this woman?
   What does she do?

   She's a writer.
   She writes books.

4. What's this woman?
   What does she do?

   She's a singer.
   She sings.

5. What's this man?
   What does he do?

   He's a waiter.
   He waits on tables.

What does Paul do for a living?		**He rides horses.**
What's he doing now?		**He's cleaning his boots.**

1. What does Marta do for a living?
   What's she doing now?

   She sings.
   She's studying a song.

2. What does Don do for a living?
   What's he doing now?

   He plays tennis.
   He's buying a racket.

3. What does Gloria do for a living?
   What's she doing now?

   She writes books.
   She's reading a letter.

4. What does Al do for a living?
   What's he doing now?

   He cooks.
   He's eating.

HOW ABOUT *YOU?*

What do *you* do? What do you *want* to do?

What are you doing now?

MR. SANDS   MR. HAMLIN

Mr. Sands gets up at 6:00. Mr. Hamlin doesn't get up at 6:00.
He doesn't get up at 7:00 either.

Mr. Sands goes to work at seven o'clock, but Mr. Hamlin doesn't.

Mr. Sands walks to work, but Mr. Hamlin doesn't walk to work.

Mr. Sands works ten hours. Mr. Hamlin doesn't work ten hours,
and he doesn't work six hours either.

In the evening Mr. Hamlin plays cards and watches TV.

Mr. Sands doesn't play cards, and he doesn't watch TV either.

1. Does Mr. Sands get up at six?
2. Does Mr. Hamlin get up at six?
3. When does Mr. Sands walk to work?
4. Does Mr. Sands work ten hours?
5. Does Mr. Hamlin work ten hours?
6. Does Mr. Sands play cards in the evening?
7. What does Mr. Hamlin do in the evening?
8. What does Mr. Sands do in the evening?

Tom likes sports cars, but he doesn't like motorcycles.

1.

2.

3.

4.

MEMORY BANK

1. comic books	2. milk	
newspapers	coffee	
3. chicken	4. tennis	
fish	backgammon	

LISTEN & UNDERSTAND

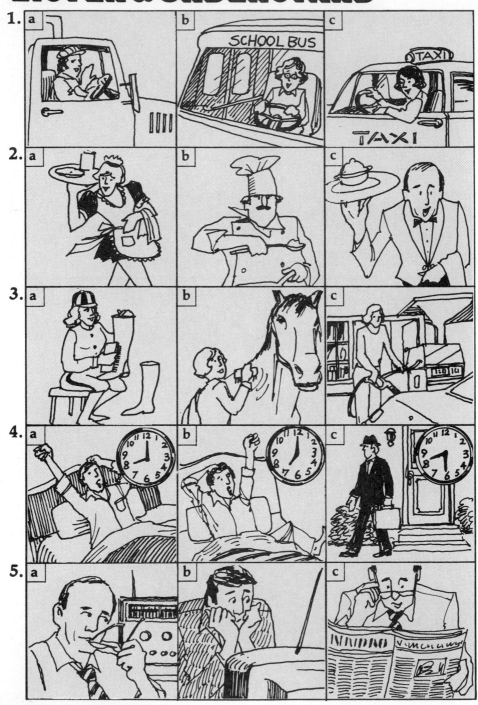

BASICS

THE SIMPLE PRESENT—THIRD-PERSON SINGULAR

STATEMENT: Tom likes sports cars, but
                                    he doesn't like motorcycles.

YES-NO QUESTION: Does s(he) play tennis?

INFORMATION QUESTION: What does s(he) do for a living?

SHORT ANSWERS: Yes, s(he) does.
                                    No, s(he) doesn't.

THE SIMPLE PRESENT AND PRESENT PROGRESSIVE

General   **Limited**
(Characteristic, habitual)   *(Temporary)*

What does he do?   What is he doing now?

He cooks.   He's eating.

CONTRACTION:

does not ⟶ doesn't

INDEFINITE ARTICLE:

She's **a** taxi driver.   She drives **a** taxi.

VOCABULARY/EXPRESSIONS

baggage	mail	truck
carry	plays	truck driver
delivers	rider	waits on
does	rides	writer
get(s) up	singer	writes
goes - *gú*	song	
golf	sports cars	do for a living
horses	studying	
hours	teach	

UNIT 3
THREE

—Do you smoke?
—No, I never smoke.
—Do you drink?
—No, I seldom drink. But....
—Well, how are you?
—I'm *fine*.
—Well, why are you here?
—I want to go to the movies with your daughter.

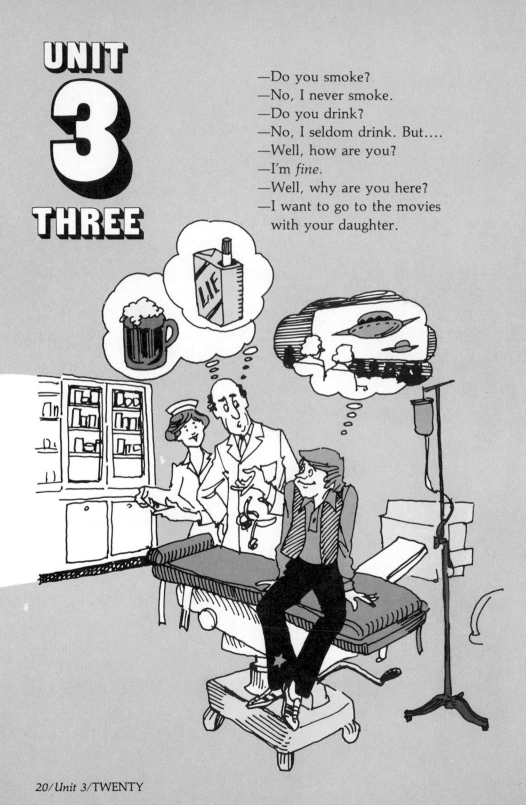

—I always get up early and
  go to bed late.
—I always get up early, too.
—*Always?*
—Well, I *usually* do.
—*Usually?*
—Well, *sometimes* I get up early.
  But I never go to bed late.
—*Never?*
—Well, I *seldom* do.

—I'm on a diet. I never have breakfast.
—Never? I always have a good breakfast.
—What do you have?
—Well, I usually have coffee and eggs.
  Sometimes I have tea and bread.
  I often have pineapple and cheese.
  And I frequently have....
—Please, stop! I'm hungry.

HOW ABOUT *YOU?*

1. Do you get up at six?
2. Do you wash in the morning?
3. Do you have eggs for breakfast?
4. Do you go to school by train?
5. Do you have fish for lunch?
6. Do you drive home from school?
7. Do you walk home from school?
8. Do you have milk for dinner?
9. Do you watch TV in the evening?
10. Do you go to bed at nine?

—My sisters always play football
after school.
—Oh, come on! Do they really?
—No, they never do. I'm joking.
—Oh. Well, *my* sisters sometimes do!

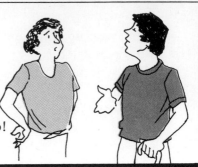

1. My cats always eat at the table.
2. My grandparents always go to the disco on Saturday night.
3. My parents always go to Alaska in winter.
4. My brothers always have candy bars for breakfast.
5. My dogs always watch TV at night.

—John usually works hard,
doesn't he?
—What? Are you joking?
He *never* works hard.
—Never?
—Well, almost never.

1. Ann usually comes on time, doesn't she?
2. Peter usually eats a big breakfast, doesn't he?
3. My sister usually looks pretty, doesn't she?
4. My teacher usually talks too much, doesn't he?
5. Ben usually likes fish, doesn't he?
6. Your mother usually cooks breakfast, doesn't she?
7. Your dog usually sleeps all afternoon, doesn't it?

HOW ABOUT *YOU?*

Now talk about things you always, usually,
never, or almost never do!

Pete goes to see his friend Charlie.

—Have a cigarette, Charlie?

—No, thanks. I never smoke now.

—What? Don't you smoke now?

—No, and I never drink either.

—Don't you ever drink?

—No, and I never go out with girls now.

—What? Don't you ever go out with girls?

—No, because I never go to parties now.

—Don't you ever go to parties?

—No, and I never stay out late.

—What? Don't you ever stay out late?

—No, never. I always get up early, swim before breakfast, play tennis after lunch and run for an hour after dinner.

Two women are talking. One says she knows a lazy man.
The other woman asks questions.

—Doesn't he always get up early?

—No, he never gets up early.

—Doesn't he always help in the house?

—No, he never helps in the house.

—Doesn't he always cook lunch?

—No, he never cooks lunch.

—Doesn't he always make the beds?

—No, he never makes the beds.

—Well, does he always sleep all Sunday?

—Yes, he always sleeps all Sunday.

—Who *is* this lazy man?

—It's my husband, of course.

Charles always gets up at seven o'clock. He goes to the bathroom and takes a shower. He shaves his face, brushes his teeth, and combs his hair. Then he goes to his bedroom and gets dressed. He takes off his bathrobe, pajamas and slippers. He puts on his underwear, his shirt and tie, his pants, and his socks and shoes. Then he goes to the kitchen and eats breakfast.

1. When does Charles get up?
2. Where does he go?
3. Does he take a shower or a bath?
4. What does he shave? Brush? Comb?
5. Then what does he do?
6. What does he take off?
7. What does he put on?
8. Then where does he go?

MRS. PARKIN IS HELPFUL

*Mr. Parkin is going to Montreal for a few days.
He doesn't like traveling, and he usually hates buying
tickets. He hates buying tickets because his wife
always "helps" him.*

MRS. PARKIN: Come on, Peter. It's your turn. Ask him when
the train leaves for Montreal.

MR. PARKIN: When does the train leave for Montreal on
Monday?

CLERK: At four in the morning.

MRS. PARKIN: That's too early, Peter. Ask him when the *next*
train leaves.

MR. PARKIN: When does the next train leave?

CLERK: At eight thirty.

MRS. PARKIN: Good, Peter. Ask him when it arrives in
Montreal.

MR. PARKIN: When does it arrive in Montreal?

CLERK: At seven in the evening.

MRS. PARKIN: Ask him if the train goes directly to Montreal.

MR. PARKIN: Does the train go directly to Montreal?

CLERK: No, you have to change trains in Toronto.

MRS. PARKIN: That's fine Peter. Ask him how much it costs.

MR. PARKIN: How much does it cost?

CLERK: A one-way ticket is fifteen dollars. Round-trip
is twenty-nine.

MRS. PARKIN: Okay, Peter, buy your ticket. Or do I always
have to do everything for you?

LISTEN & UNDERSTAND

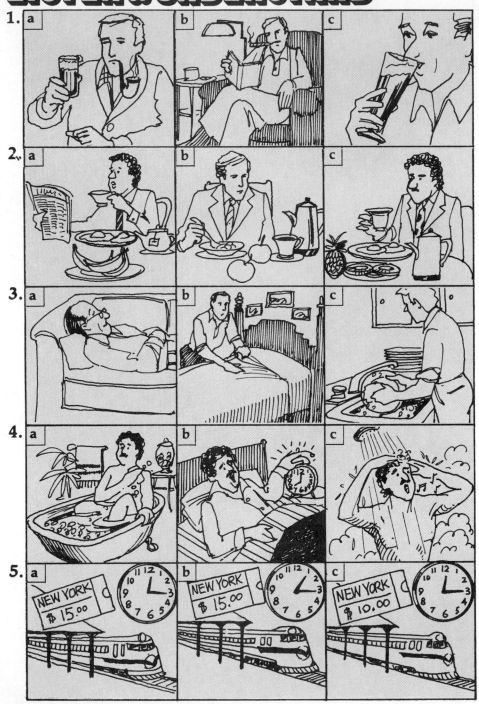

PRONUNCIATION

I.

nurse	skirt	sir	girl
her	shirt	first	work
purple	service	church	circles

Yes, sir. The girl can go to church.

A nurse can't work in a purple skirt.

II.

cousin	nuts	son	brother
what	color	under	mother
summer	husband	brush	but

What color are nuts?

My mother is buying my brother a brush.

III.

who	shoes	do	movies
boots	school	scooter	too

Who goes to the movies at noon?

Do they like school too?

IV.

book	look	football	cook
woman	good	foot	put

That woman is a good cook.

Look! Here's your book.

V. Do they have to go to school this summer?

That woman is a good nurse.

What color is your husband's shirt?

I work in a service station.

Do the ladies like my skirt with these shoes?

BASICS

ADVERBS:

He	frequently often always sometimes usually	gets up early.

She	seldom almost never never	works hard.

THIRD-PERSON -S FORM:

He gets dressed in the morning.

She eats breakfast.

It sleeps all afternoon.

NEGATIVE QUESTION FORMS:

Don't you ever go to parties?
Doesn't he always make the beds?
Ann usually comes on time, doesn't she?

VERB HAVE (TO EAT/DRINK):

I usually have coffee for breakfast.

VOCABULARY/EXPRESSIONS

almost	lazy	ticket
always	leave(s)	too
ask	never	turn
bath	often	underwear
because	one-way	usually
cigarette	pajamas	
cost(s)	parties	I'm joking.
directly	really	Oh, come on!
ever	round-trip	on a diet
everything	seldom	on time
frequently	shave(s)	put(s) on
gets dressed	smoke	stay out
hard	sometimes	take(s) a shower
hungry	then	take(s) off

TEST YOURSELF

I.

1. Do you like tea? Yes, I
   a) always
   b) never   drink tea.
   c) seldom

2. Do you like milk? No, so I
   a) always
   b) never   drink milk.
   c) sometimes

3. Do you have a backgammon board?
   Yes, so I
   a) never
   b) seldom   play.
   c) often

4. Does Tom drink milk?
   a) Yes, he does.
   b) Yes, he doesn't.
   c) No, he does.

5. Does Pam smoke?
   a) No, she does.
   b) No, she doesn't.
   c) Yes, she doesn't.

6. You have to hurry.
   No I don't. I'm not
   a) early.
   b) late.
   c) directly.

7. Do you want to play tennis?
   a) In my room.
   b) Yes, I do.
   c) In the afternoon.

8. When do you want to sail?
   a) In my room.
   b) Yes, I do.
   c) In the afternoon.

9. Where do you want to study?
   a) In my room.
   b) Yes, I do.
   c) In the afternoon.

II.

1. — Can she dance?
   — Yes,...now.

2. — Can she play table tennis?
   — Yes,...now.

3. — Can he cook?
   — Yes,...now.

4. — Can he sing?
   — Yes,...now.

5. What does Tom do for a living?
   What's he doing now?

6. What does Zelda do for a living?
   What's she doing now?

III.

1. Where do you want to go?
   I want....

2. How do you come to school?
   I come....

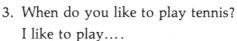

3. When do you like to play tennis?
   I like to play....

4. When do you want to have lunch?
   ....

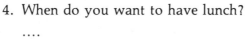

5. When do you usually go to sleep?
   I....

What does Mary do every morning?  She brushes her teeth.

1. What does Tom do before dinner?  He washes his hands.

2. What does he do every morning?  He changes the baby.

3. What does Mr. Jones do after work?  He waxes his car.

4. What does the cat do?  It chases mice.

5. What does a teacher do?  She teaches.

6. What does a dancer do?  He dances.

What does he clean?  **He cleans the windows.**

1. What does she open?  She opens the mail.

2. What does he find? He finds a dollar.

3. What does she speak?  She speaks Spanish.

4. What does he lift?  He lifts the baby.

5. What does she write?  She writes music.

6. What does it eat? It eats bananas.

I hate winter. I hate to go to work. The alarm clock rings. I run into the bathroom, brush my teeth, wash my hands and face, run into the kitchen, drink a cup of coffee, dress in the bedroom, kiss my wife good-bye, run to my car, push it to start it, crash into the gate, chase the bus and miss it.... It's the same every year when the snow comes!

The alarm clock rings. What does the man do?
He runs into the bathroom,
brushes his teeth,....

What does Tom carry?  **He carries the mail.**

1. What does she fly? She flies a plane.

2. What does he dry? He dries the dishes.

3. Where does she hurry every day? She hurries to school.

4. What does he empty? He empties the trash.

5. What does she try to read?  She tries to read a book.

MR. JENKINS'S DAY

It is seven-thirty in the morning. Mr. Jenkins gets out of bed. He goes into the bathroom and washes. He dries his hands and face on the towel and then brushes his teeth. Then he dresses. He puts on his shirt and pants, shoes and socks, and his tie. Then he puts on his hat and jacket. Mr. Jenkins is a mail carrier, and he wears a uniform. At quarter past eight he kisses his wife and children good-bye. He's late this morning.

The bus comes at twenty past eight. Mr. Jenkins hurries to the bus stop. He sees the bus. He runs and tries to catch the bus, but he misses it. He waits for the next bus. He's late for work. It is raining, and there is a puddle next to the bus stop. When the bus comes, it splashes Mr. Jenkins.

Mr. Jenkins carries a mailbag. It is very heavy today, because there is a lot of mail. At four o'clock he opens the gate of the last house. He's very tired. A dog comes out of the house and chases Mr. Jenkins.

"Oh," cries Mr. Jenkins. "What a day!"

1. What does Mr. Jenkins do at seven-thirty?
2. What does he put on?
3. What does he do at quarter past eight?
4. Is it raining?
5. What does the bus do?
6. What does Mr. Jenkins carry?
7. What does he do at four?
8. What does the dog do?

What does s(he) do every day?

1.

2.

3.

4.

What do they do every day?

1.

2.

3.

4.

MEMORY BANK

1. opens the mail   2. carries the mail
     3. changes the baby   4. drives a taxi

1. dry the dishes   2. make their bed
     3. watch TV   4. play tennis

THE DIRTY FAMILY

1. I have dirty hands.

Of course. You never wash your hands.

2. You have a dirty face.

Of course. I never wash my face.

3. Tom has dirty knees.

Of course. He never washes his knees.

4. Lucy has dirty hair.

Of course. She never washes her hair.

5. You and Henry have dirty toes.

Of course. We never wash our toes.

6. Bill and Barbara have dirty elbows.

Of course. They never wash their elbows.

7. My brother and I have dirty ears.

Of course. You never wash your ears.

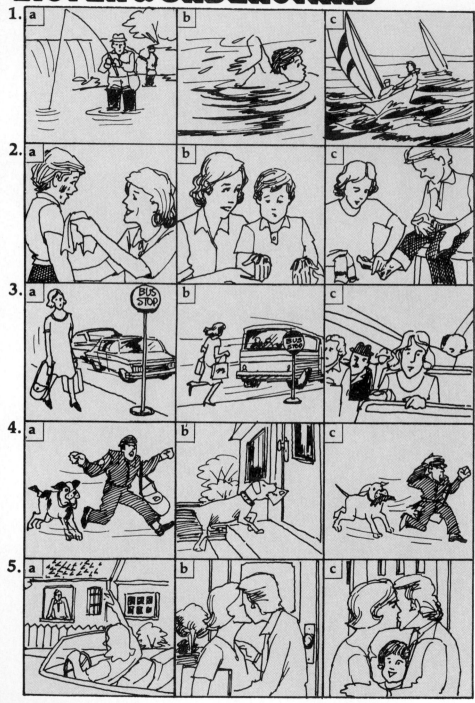

THE SIMPLE PRESENT TENSE

THIRD PERSON SINGULAR:

[-S]		[-Z]		[-IZ]	
cook	cooks	arrive	arrives	brush	brushes
cost	costs	clean	cleans	change	changes
drink	drinks	comb	combs	chase	chases
eat	eats	come	comes	crash	crashes
get up	gets up	deliver	delivers	dance	dances
help	helps	drive	drives	dress	dresses
lift	lifts	find	finds	kiss	kisses
like	likes	leave	leaves	miss	misses
make	makes	open	opens	push	pushes
put on	puts on	play	plays	teach	teaches
sleep	sleeps	run	runs	wash	washes
speak	speaks	see	sees	watch	watches
take off	takes off	shave	shaves		
talk	talks				
wait	waits				
walk	walks				
work	works				
write	writes				

Y/IES FORMS

carry	carries	empty	empties	hurry	hurries
dry	dries	fly	flies	try to	tries to

VOCABULARY/EXPRESSIONS

alarm clock	mail carrier	start
bag	mice	towel
catch	mirror	trash
dancer	of	uniform
dirty	plane	waxes
dishes	puddle	
dries	rings	comes out of
gate	same	gets out of
hate (to)	smiles	Ugh!
heavy	snow	What a day!
into	splashes	

UNIT 5 FIVE

—Are you going to help me?
—No, I'm not.
—Are you going to wash the car?
—No, I'm not.
—Are you going to clean the yard?
—No, I'm not.
—What *are* you going to do?
—I'm going to sleep. I'm tired!

—Where's **John** going next **summer?**
—**He's** going to **England.**
—Oh, really?
—Yes, **he** goes there every **summer.**

1. Mary 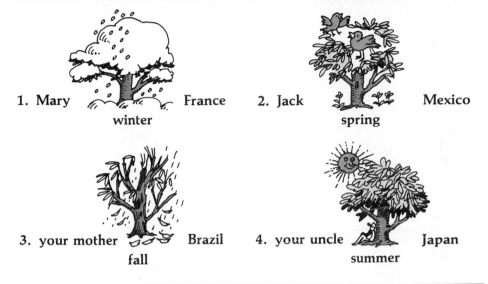 France   2. Jack   Mexico
   winter   spring

3. your mother   Brazil   4. your uncle   Japan
   fall   summer

—Where are John and Jane going?
—They're going to **the United States.**
—Oh, really?
—Yes, they go there **every fall.**

1. Where are Fred and Judy going?   **Turkey, every spring**
2. Where are Tom and Bill going?   **Singapore, every winter**
3. Where are they going?   **Colombia, every summer**
4. Where are the Jenkins going?   **Mexico, every fall**
5. Where are your parents going?   **Spain, every March**
6. Where are they going?   **Peru, every year**
7. Where are your aunt and uncle   **Canada, every August**
   going?
8. Where are your cousins going?   **Greece, every September**

I am going to sleep.

I	**am**		get dressed.
			make the beds.
He			sing.
She	**is**		play soccer.
It			sleep.
		going to	eat.
We			walk.
You	**are**		run.
They			have dinner.
			work.

We are going to eat.

1. They	cook lunch.
	watch TV.
2. I	clean the yard.
	run.
3. He	ride a horse.
	take a bath.
4. She	study.
	turn on the light.
5. You	swim.
	stop now.

HOW ABOUT *YOU?*
1. What are you going to do tomorrow?
2. What are you going to do tonight?
3. What are you going to do next week?
4. Where are you going on Saturday?
   What are you going to do there?
5. Where are you going next summer?
   What are you going to do there?

TELEPHONE CONVERSATION

—Hello, Bob. Are you **eating lunch** now?
—No, I'm not. Are you?
—Yes, because I'm going to **watch TV** later.

1. working/play football
2. cleaning your room/dance at the disco
3. doing your homework/listen to the radio
4. having dinner/wash my hair
5. reading/listen to my records
6. studying/listen to the concert
7. helping in the kitchen/swim
8. getting dressed/wash the car

What are they going to do?

What are they going to do?

1. Bill sits down with the newspaper.
   He's going to ....
2. Jill has a tennis racket in her hand.
3. Mary is asleep. The alarm clock rings.
4. Jane sits down with a pen in her hand.
5. Jeff sits down in front of the TV.
6. Frank and Gloria turn on the record player.
7. My grandmother puts on her bathing suit.
8. Uncle Mario has a table-tennis paddle.
9. My sister opens a cookbook.
10. Juan has a very dirty car.

Where *are they going?*	*When* *are they going?*	*How* *are they going?*

CAROL WINTERS

I talked to Carol Winters, the famous movie star, at her hotel this morning.

—Good morning, Miss Winters. What are you going to do today?

—Well, first I'm going to swim in the pool for half an hour, and then I'm going to have breakfast at ten o'clock with my producer Frank Zinc. Then the photographers are going to take pictures for a newspaper. In the afternoon I'm going to go shopping. I'm going to try on some new clothes for my next movie. Then I am going to sleep for one or two hours after five o'clock, because at seven o'clock I'm going to have dinner with a good friend. We are going to go dancing at the King Club...(but I hope you aren't going to write that in your newspaper. We're only good friends.). And then I'm going to bed at about eleven o'clock.

—You're going to bed early?

—Of course, I can't work *all* the time!

What is Carol Winters going to do?

LISTEN & UNDERSTAND

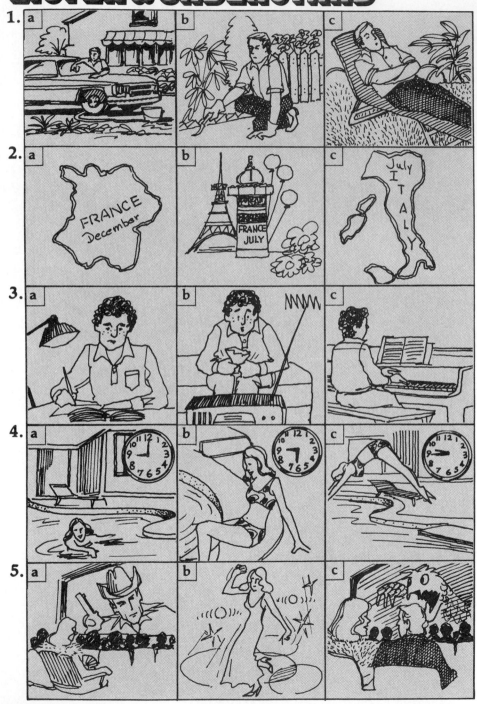

PRONUNCIATION

I. bathrobe   elbow   number   September
    bus   bathroom   breakfast   baseball
    bed   boyfriend   bank   buy
    bicycle   but   beef   beans
    boots   blouse   blue   behind

   My boyfriend's bicycle is behind the bank.

   Bob is buying beef and beans.

II. people   happy   shopping   newspaper
    please   pretty   sleep   grandparents
    polish   pineapple   pajamas   police officer
    play   pilot   type   purple
    peaches   lamp   piano   put

   The police officer and the pilot are playing the piano.

   Pam is putting on purple pajamas.

III. Peter is buying peaches, beans, pineapples and beef.

    Pam's blue blouse is pretty.

    Bill is playing baseball with Paul and Bob.

    Please polish Ben's boots.

    My bedroom is purple, but the lamp is blue.

    Victor is buying very blue boots.

    Vera is eating a very big banana.

    Bob is on vacation in Venezuela.

    I have bread for breakfast.

    Veronica and Ben are very late.

    I'm going to take the bus to the village.

BASICS

GO + NOUN/GO + VERB:

He	is			England.
She		going	to	Mexico.
We				Canada.
You	are			
They				

He	is		study.
She		going to	read.
We			
You	are		work.
They			

Where is he going? ——————→ He is going to England.

What is he going to do? ——→ He is going to study.

WORD ORDER :

	Time	**Place**
He goes	there	every summer.

USES OF THE PRESENT TENSES :

Time	**Tense**
He **brushes** his teeth (every day).	Simple Present
He **is brushing** his teeth (now).	Present Progressive
He **is going to brush** his teeth (tomorrow).	Present Progressive (future)
She **is going** to England (next summer).	Present Progressive (future)

VOCABULARY/EXPRESSIONS

about	hope	pool	all the time
asleep	horse	producer	getting dressed
bathing suit	later	ship	go dancing
first	light	sits down	go shopping
has	movie star	try on	take pictures
having	photographers	turn on	

TEST YOURSELF

I. At seven o'clock the alarm clock

rings.
hurries.
works.

Sam gets out

of bed and

lifts
chases
walks

to the bathroom and

washes
brushes
tries

his face.

Then he

dresses.
misses.
crashes

He puts on his blue

bag.
snow.
uniform.

Then he eats breakfast and

chases
hurries
kisses

to school. He

pushes
opens
carries

his books in the book bag. After school he

changes
helps
dresses

his clothes and

delivers
plays
splashes

football. In the evening

he

hurries
opens
watches

TV.

II. 1. What does he clean?   He . . . . . . the windows.

2. What does he carry?   He . . . . . . a bag.

3. What does he push?   He . . . . . . his car.

4. What does she put on?   She . . . . . . her pajamas.

5. What does she write?   She . . . . . . books.

6. What does she fly?   She . . . . . . a plane.

7. What does it chase?   It . . . . mice.

III.
1. Do the boys like to study? Yes, they ... their homework now.
2. Does Fred like TV? Yes, he ... TV every day.
3. Is Mary washing her hair? No, she ... her hair later.
4. Are they going to watch TV? No, Mary ... do her homework, and Bob ... read.
5. ... Jack going next summer? He's going to London.
6. ... Pam going to Greece? She's going next spring.
7. Does Mrs. Stone want to go to France? Yes, she's ... there next fall.

IV.
1. Where .... ?

She's going to study in the library.

2. When .... ?

It rings at seven o'clock.

3. What's Bill doing?

He's ....

4. What's Tom going to do?

He's ....

5. What's Sally going to do?

She's ....

6. ..... next summer?

To France. She goes to France every summer.

7. Is Mr. Mitchell going to walk to work?

No. He's going to take a taxi. ..... raining.

—Did you lock the doors and windows?
—Of course I did.
—Did you stop the newspaper?
—Yes, I did.
—Did you pack the travel books?
—Yes, yes, of course I did.
—Do you have the tickets?
—What? No. Don't *you* have them?
—Of course I do. I'm only joking.
—Ha. Very funny.

—Do you want my **lemonade?**

—Yes, thank you.

—Okay, here you are.

What's the matter? Don't you want to **drink** it?

—No, thank you. I don't.

EAT	DRINK	READ
1.	2.	3.
4.	5.	6.
7.	8.	9.

—Do you want **John's coat**?

—Doesn't **he** want it?

—No, **he** doesn't.

—Okay, I'll take it.

1. Mary's

2. my father's

3. my uncle's

4. my brother's

5. grandmother's

6. my mother's

7. Sam's

8. Dick's

MEMORY BANK

1. dress	2. book	3. hat
4. tie		5. sweater
6. sandwich	7. ice cream	8. newspaper

Did he type a letter?  **Yes, he did.**

1. Did she lock the door?  Yes, she did.

2. Did he put on his jacket? Yes, she did.

No, he didn't.

3. Did they play at eight?  No, they didn't.

4. Did she wash her clothes?  Yes, she did.

5. Did he wax his car? Yes, he did.

6. Did they clean their room? No, they didn't.

7. Did the bus splash them?  Yes, it did.

GOING ON VACATION

Mr. Carter packs his clothes. He closes his suitcase. He carries it to the front door. Then he looks back at the living room. The window is open. He closes it. Then he sees some books on a chair. He picks them up and packs them in a bag.

5   He stops and listens. The radio is still on. He switches it off. "That's everything," he thinks. He opens the front door, goes out, and locks the door behind him.

Mrs. Carter is waiting on the sidewalk.

"Where's the taxi?" she asks.

10   "Taxi?" Mr. Carter answers.

"Yes, the *taxi*. Didn't you call a taxi?"

"Well, no."

Mrs. Carter sighs. "Give me the key," she says.

Mrs. Carter goes into the house. She hears something

15 upstairs. She rushes up to the bathroom. It's full of water! She turns off the water and cleans up the floor. "That's everything," she thinks. She goes outside.

"You're hopeless," she says to her husband. "You didn't turn off the water!"

20   "Oh, sorry. Well, where's the taxi?"

"Taxi?"

"Yes, the *taxi*. Didn't you call a taxi?"

| Did | Mr. Carter | pack a suitcase? close the window? go upstairs? pack the books? | Yes, | he she | did. |
| | Mrs. Carter | call a taxi? turn off the water? lock the door? clean up the floor? turn off the radio? | No, | he she | didn't. |

THE ACCIDENT

A policeman asks you a lot of questions about the accident.
Answer the questions with:

Yes, he did.   **Yes, it did.**

No, he didn't.   **No, it didn't.**

Yes, I did.   **Yes, I do.**

No, I didn't.   **I'm sorry. I don't know.**

1. Did the car drive onto the sidewalk?

. . . .

2. Did the driver see the boy sitting on the sidewalk?

. . . .

3. Did you call the police?

. . . .

4. Did you call for an ambulance?

. . . .

5. Did the driver wait for the police?

. . . .

6. Did you see the driver's face?

. . . .

7. Did you write down the license number?

. . . .

Thank you.

HOW ABOUT *YOU?* *Answer* Yes, I did. *or* No, I didn't.

    1. Did you play tennis yesterday?
    2. Did you get up at seven today?
    3. Did you see your uncle last week?
    4. Did you listen to records last night?
    5. Did you go to the disco last Saturday?
    6. Did you do your homework?

ON YOUR OWN

Work with a friend. Practice asking and answering questions from the box. Use Yes, I do/No, I don't.
    Yes, s(he) does.
    No, s(he) doesn't.
    Yes, I did.
    No, I didn't. (etc.)

Do	I you we they	study play tennis go dancing	every day?
		get up early	
Does	he she it	make lunch eat fish drink milk	
		read the newspaper	
Did	I you we they he she it	get dressed watch TV go to school work go shopping fly to France	today? last night? yesterday? last week? last year? this morning?

LISTEN & UNDERSTAND

BASICS

AUXILIARIES: DO/DID

Do	I you we they	drink milk?	Yes,	I you we they	do.	No,	I you we they	don't.
Does	he she it	drink milk?	Yes,	he she it	does.	No,	he she it	doesn't.
Did	I you we they he she it	drink milk?	Yes,	I you we they he she it	did.	No,	I you we they he she it	didn't.

CONTRACTION:

did not ⟶ didn't

VOCABULARY/EXPRESSIONS

ambulance	hears	pack(s)	thinks
answers	hopeless	picks up	travel books
cake	know	rushes	turn(s) off
call	key	says	up
close(s)	license	sidewalk	upstairs
did	lock(s)	sighs	yesterday
door(s)	onto	something	
front	open	suitcase	Ha.
full of	outside	switches off	I'll take it!

UNIT 7 SEVEN

—Dad, can I have five dollars?
—Well, I don't know.
  Did you clean your room?
—No, Anna cleaned my room.
—Did you wash the car?
—No, Anna washed the car.
—Did you paint the gate?
—No, Anna painted the gate.
—Well, then this five dollars
  is for Anna!

[-d]

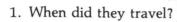

1. When did they travel? 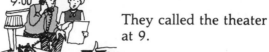 They traveled at 7 in the morning.

2. When did they arrive?  They arrived at 8.

3. When did they call the theater?  They called the theater at 9.

4. When did they return? They returned at midnight.

—Did you **clean your room?**
—No, I didn't **clean** it.
—Why not?
—Max **cleaned** it instead.

1. change the tire/changed

2. close the window/closed

3. deliver the box/delivered

4. play the piano/played

5. iron your dress/ironed

6. call the theater/called

1. What did she dry?  She dried her hair.

2. Where did she hurry?  She hurried to the church.

3. What did she worry about? She worried about the rings.

4. Who did she marry? She married Fred.

THE FRED FRUMPS

—Did you **copy the lesson**?
—No, I didn't.
—Why not?
—Betty **copied** it instead.

1. **empty the trash/emptied**

2. **try my cake/tried**

3. **dry my bathing suit/dried**

4. **fry the fish/fried**

5. **carry the box/carried**

6. **worry about the weather/worried about**

[-t]

1. Where did he work? He worked in an office.

2. What did he miss? He missed the bus.

3. Where did he park? He parked in front of the bank.

4. What did he type? He typed a letter.

5. Who did he kiss? He kissed his girl friend.

—Did you **wash the clothes?**
—No, Mary **washed** them for me.

---

1. type the letters/typed

2. cook the beans/cooked

3. brush the dogs/brushed

4. watch the children/watched

5. polish my shoes/polished

6. wax the floors/waxed

[-id]

1. What did they want?  They wanted a house.

2. What did they rent?  They rented an apartment.

3. What did they paint? They painted the walls.

4. What did they plant?  They planted a tree.

5. What did they wait for? They waited for summer.

6. What did they hate?  They hated the cold nights.

THE BIRTHDAY

It was my father's birthday yesterday. My mother baked a cake. She didn't have any candles, so she hurried to the store.

My father arrived home at four-thirty. He opened the kitchen door and looked at the birthday cake. Then he picked it up and
5 walked to the back yard. He waited and waited for my mother.

Finally, two hours later, my mother returned. My father waved to her from the yard. My mother looked upset and worried.

"Hi, what's the matter?" my father called.

10 "Oh, I baked a cake for you, but I didn't have any candles. I looked in four stores, and they didn't have any candles, either."

"No candles?"

"No candles."

15 My father pointed to the cake plate. It was empty.

"Don't worry...no cake!"

1. What did she bake?
2. Where did she hurry to?
3. When did the father arrive home?
4. What did he open?
5. What did he look at?
6. What did he pick up?
7. Where did he walk to?
8. When did the mother return?
9. How did she look?
10. What did she say?
11. What did the father point to?
12. What did he say?

Anna worked very hard all day. At four,
she called her roommate, Jane.

ANNA: Hi, Jane. What did you do today?

JANE: Well, first I *cleaned* my room.

ANNA: Did you clean my room too?

JANE: Yes, I did. Then I *waxed* my floor.

ANNA: Did you wax my floor too?

JANE: Yes, I did. Then I *emptied* my wastebaskets.

ANNA: Did you empty my wastebaskets too?

JANE: Yes, I did. Then I *shortened* my skirt.

ANNA: Did you shorten my skirt too?

JANE: Yes, I did. Then I *cooked* my dinner.

ANNA: Did you cook my dinner, too?

JANE: Yes, I did.

ANNA: Oh, you're a good roommate, Jane.

JANE: Thanks. But there's one thing I didn't tell you.

I *burned* your dinner, too!

What did they do yesterday?

1.

2.

3.

4.

5.

6.

7.

8.

9. Hello, Jane?

10. RENT

MEMORY BANK

1. watched TV   2. typed a letter   3. played tennis
        4. dried the dishes   5. painted a chair
6. changed a tire   7. baked a cake   8. copied the lesson
        9. called Jane   10. rented a house

WHAT ABOUT *YOU?*
    What did you do yesterday? Last week? Last Year?

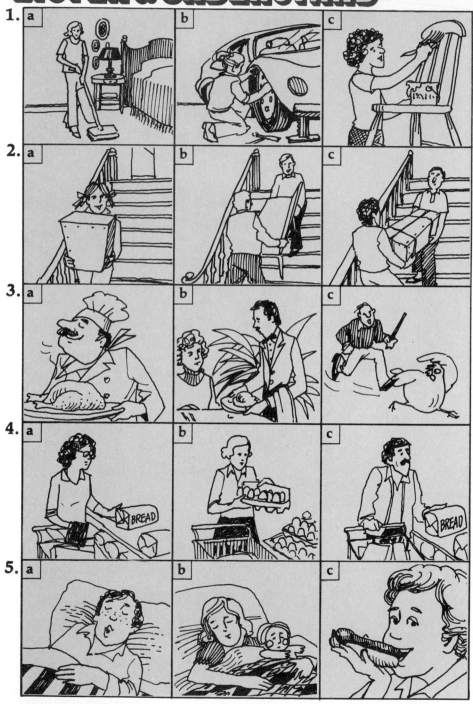

PRONUNCIATION

I. water   well   sidewalk   woman
    housewife   want   we   watch
    sandwich   homework   wear   always

      My wife wanted to work.

      Well, we wear boots in the water.

II. drive   travel   movie   ever
     five   very   never   arrive
     heavy   TV   leave   village

      Tom never drives to the movies.

      Mr. Paine is going to deliver the TV at five.

III. yard   yesterday   your   uniform
      you   yes   yellow   use

      Did you play in the yard yesterday?

      Yes, my uniform is yellow.

IV. enjoy   jacket   jeans   bridge
     change   village   Japan   joking

      Does John have to change his jacket and jeans?

      Jack enjoyed the village in Japan.

V. Jill is wearing your yellow pajamas.

    The woman arrived in Japan yesterday.

    Yes, we traveled to the village to watch TV.

    John never wears your yellow jacket.

    We can leave your uniform with John's wife.

BASICS

THE SIMPLE PAST TENSE

STATEMENTS: Anna cleaned my room.
                     They didn't have any candles.

INFORMATION QUESTION: When did they arrive?

[-d]			[-t]	
arrive	arrived		bake	baked
call	called		brush	brushed
change	changed		cook	cooked
clean	cleaned		dress	dressed
close	closed		kiss	kissed
deliver	delivered		look	looked
iron	ironed		miss	missed
open	opened		park	parked
play	played		pick up	picked up
return	returned		polish	polished
shorten	shortened		type	typed
travel	traveled		walk	walked
y ⟶ ied			wash	washed
carry	carried		watch	watched
copy	copied		wax	waxed
dry	dried		**[-id]**	
empty	emptied		hate	hated
fry	fried		paint	painted
hurry	hurried		plant	planted
marry	married		point	pointed
try	tried		rent	rented
worry	worried		wait	waited
			want	wanted

VOCABULARY/EXPRESSIONS

any	candles	roommate	walls
apartment	empty	said	was
back	finally	tell	wastebaskets
birthday	instead	tire	waved
box	lesson	tree	worried
burned	rings	upset	

TEST YOURSELF

I. 1. Is this your raincoat?   No, it's   **a)** Tom.
                                                        b) Tom's.
                                                        c) of Tom.

                                                    a) Yes, I do.
   2. Did you clean your room? **b)** No, I didn't.
                                                    c) No, I don't.

      a) Where
   3. **b)** What did they arrive? At nine.
      c) When

      a) Do
   4. **b)** Does John come?   Yes, he did.
      c) Did

        a) do
   5. When **b)** does Peter study? Every day.
        c) did

        a) do
   6. How **b)** does Mary travel? She traveled by car.
        c) did

      a) Do
   7. **b)** Does they always eat No, they sometimes eat at eight.
      c) Did   at seven?

      a) Do
   8. **b)** Does Pam like Peter? Yes, and he likes her, too.
      c) Did

                                                     a) or at nine?
   9. Does the movie start at eight **b)** at nine?   At eight.
                                                     c) nine?

II.

1. Do you want my lemonade?   Don't you want....drink it?
2. Did you play football yesterday?   Yes, I......
3. Did John go to school yesterday?   No, he......
4. Do you want my coffee?   Thanks, but....you want it?
5. Do you want Bill's tea?   OK, but....he want it?
6. ....Henry wear a raincoat?   Yes, he did.
7. Did Mr. Jake open the door?   No, Mrs. Jake....it.
8. Did you shorten your skirt?   No, Sally....it instead.
9. Did she dry the dishes?   No, she....her hair.
10. ....?   I arrived at nine.
11. ....?   He parked the car.
12. ....?   She kissed her sister.

13. What did Ann do?   She........her skirt.

14. What did Sue do?   She........the trash.

15. What did Tom do?   He........a letter.

16. What did she want?   She....a.....

17. What did he wax?   He....the.....

18. What did they plant?   They....a.....

19. What did she watch?   She.... .....

20. What did he carry?   He....a.....

John was at an "adult" movie. Now his mother is very angry.

1. Were you and Walter there?	No, we weren't.
2. Were you and Jack there?	No, we weren't.
3. Were Max and George there?	No, they weren't.
4. Were you there with Pat?	No, I wasn't.
5. Were you there with Alice?	No, I wasn't.
6. Was Nancy there with you?	No, she wasn't.
7. Was Sam there with you?	No, he wasn't.
8. Were you there alone?	No, I wasn't.
9. Well, who was with you?	Father was!

I		
He		
She	**was**	
The dog		
		there last night.
We		
You	**were**	
They		

Last night Susan was at a party.
She calls Maria to tell her about it.

SUSAN: Hello, Maria? This is Susan.

MARIA: Hi, Susan. Did you go to the party last night?

SUSAN: Yes, I did. Why weren't you there?

MARIA: Oh, I was too tired.

SUSAN: That's too bad. It was a good party.

MARIA: Was Peter there?

SUSAN: Oh yes. He was dancing all evening!

MARIA: Was Gloria there?

SUSAN: Yes, she was dancing with Peter.
I think she was kissing him, too!

MARIA: *What?* Peter was kissing Gloria?

SUSAN: Uhh, I didn't say *that*, Maria.
Listen, I have to go shopping now. Bye.

Susan knows that Maria is angry.
She calls Peter.

SUSAN: Hello, Peter? This is Susan.

PETER: Hi, Susan. Did you have a good time last night?

SUSAN: Yes, I did. Did *you?*

PETER: Yes, I guess so. But I really missed Maria.

SUSAN: Well, I just talked to her, Peter.
She knows you were dancing with Gloria.

PETER: Oh no.

SUSAN: Oh yes. And she knows you were kissing Gloria, too.

PETER: Oh, I wasn't! Gloria was kissing *me!*

SUSAN: Well, tell *that* to Maria.

PETER: I'm going to call her right away.
Hang up, Susan.

SUSAN: Bye, Peter. Good luck!

Peter is going to call Maria. She's going to ask him these questions. What do you think Peter is going to say?

1. Did you like the party last night?
2. Did you dance with all the girls?
3. Was Gloria there?
4. Were you dancing with Gloria?
5. Were you kissing Gloria?
6. Did you really miss me?

Change **is** *to* **was** *and* **are** *to* **were.**

There is a party at Mario's house. There are eighteen people there. Bill and Liz are playing the piano. Sally is singing. Peter is dancing with all the girls. Susan is watching Gloria. Gloria is dancing with Peter, but Peter is thinking about Maria.

Fill in with **is, are, was** *or* **were.**

When I was a student there...many horses, but there...not many cars. There...only one man in the village with a car. Now there...many cars, but there ...only one horse.
There...an old woman in our village. She rides the horse to the village every day. She says, "There...no traffic when I was a girl."

| What were they doing when you arrived? | They were jogging. |

1.
2.
3.

4.
5.
6.

7.
8.
9.

10.
11.
12.

MEMORY BANK

1. watching TV
2. playing chess
3. singing
4. swimming
5. kissing
6. washing the dishes
7. reading
8. drinking
9. eating
10. sleeping
11. dancing
12. playing cards

—Are they **reading** now?
—I don't think so.
  At least they weren't **reading** when I was there.

1.
2.
3.

4.
5.
6.

—Is **she working** now?
—I don't think so.
  At least **she** wasn't **working** when I was there.

1.
2.
3.

4.
5.
6.

MEMORY BANK

1. watching	2. eating	3. washing
4. singing	5. playing	6. cooking
1. sleeping	2. studying	3. typing
4. ironing	5. jogging	6. painting

LISTEN & UNDERSTAND

BASICS

TO BE:

	Present	Past
I	am	was
He She It	is	was
You We They	are	were

THERE + TO BE:

there is   there was
there are   there were

CONTRACTIONS:

was not ⟶ wasn't   were not ⟶ weren't

SIMPLE PAST: (completed action)

What did you do?   I danced.

PAST PROGRESSIVE: (during the past)

What were you doing?   I was dancing.

What were they doing when you arrived?   They were dancing.

She wasn't working when I was there.
They weren't reading when I was there.

VOCABULARY/EXPRESSIONS

alone	at least	I guess so.
ironing	Good luck!	That's too bad.
jogging	Hang up.	
were	have a good time	
writing	I don't think so.	

—Do you want to go to the rock concert with me?
—Sure. When is it?
—The first of next month.
—Uh oh. Is the first a Thursday?
—Yes, it is.
—I'm sorry, I can't go.
  I always play tennis on Thursday.

SUN.	MON.	TUES.	WED.	THURS.	FRI.	SAT.
1 first	2 second	3 third	4 fourth	5 fifth	6 sixth	7 seventh
8 eighth	9 ninth	10 tenth	11 eleventh	12 twelfth	13 thirteenth	14 fourteenth
15 fifteenth	16 sixteenth	17 seventeenth	18 eighteenth	19 nineteenth	20 twentieth	21 twenty-first
22 twenty-second	23 twenty-third	24 twenty-fourth	25 twenty-fifth	26 twenty-sixth	27 twenty-seventh	28 twenty-eighth
29 twenty-ninth	30 thirtieth	31 thirty-first				

This is Monty Mick's calendar for next month.
Monty is a rock singer.

S	M	T	W	T	F	S
	1	3 p.m. 2 DETROIT	3	4	4:00 5 NEW YORK	6
7	8 HOUSTON	9	10	10 p.m. 11 DALLAS	12 Patty	13
14 Alice	15	16	8 p.m. 17 LONDON	18	19	20
21	22 PARIS	23	24 Mary Lou	25	9:30 26 MEXICO CITY	27
28	29 Mom's birthday	30 Recording date	31 MONTREAL			

1. When is he going to sing in Detroit?   On Tuesday the second.
   What time is he going to sing?   At three in the afternoon.
2. When is he going to sing in London?
   What time?
3. When is he going to meet Alice?
4. When is he going to sing in Mexico City?
   What time?
5. When is his mother's birthday?
6. When is he going to date Mary Lou?
7. When is he going to sing in Dallas?
   What time?
8. When is he going to see Patty?
9. When is he going to sing in New York?
   What time?
10. When is he going to record a song?

Peter 6/7/1943

Peter was born on June the seventh, nineteen forty-three.

1. Aurora	10/27/1940	4. Alma	2/8/1955
2. Frank	5/20/1925	5. Alex	12/11/1961
3. Maureen	1/14/1893	6. Sid	3/6/1848

When was he born?		**In fifteen sixty-four.**
When did he die?	William Shakespeare	**In sixteen sixteen.**
How long did he live?	1564-1616	**For fifty-two years.**

1.

1935-1977
Elvis Presley

2.

1867-1934
Marie Curie

3.

1881-1973
Pablo Picasso

4.
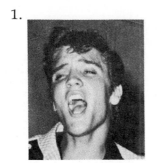

1917-1963
John F. Kennedy

5.

1880-1968
Helen Keller

6.

1770-1827
Ludwig van Beethoven

Mr. and Mrs. Walter P. O'Rourke
request the honour of your presence
at the marriage of their daughter
Kathleen Marie
to
Arthur G. Proctor
on Saturday, the ninth of September
nineteen hundred and seventy-eight
at seven-thirty in the evening
St. Theresa's Church
63 Winter Street
North Reading, Massachusetts

R.S.V.P.

It's a boy!
ROBERT
"Bobby"
BUMPY, Jr.

Nov. 18
3: a.m.
8 lbs.
4 oz.

Come and see us!
Bob + Mary Bumpy
161 Fisher St.

Party

Date *Friday, Dec. 14, 1979*

Time *5 - 7 p.m.*

Place *Meg & Jim Weston's*

1. When was Kathleen married?
2. What day was the party on?
3. What time was the Bumpy baby born?
4. Where was the wedding?
5. Who was giving the party?
6. When was Bobby born?
7. When did the party start?
8. How much did Bobby weigh?
9. How long did the party last?
10. Who was announcing the birth?

A DRIVE ON THE MOON

The first Americans landed on the moon in 1969. They walked. In 1971 Scott and Irwin in *Apollo 15* had a Moon Rover. At half past nine on Saturday morning David Scott climbed out of his spaceship, *The Falcon.* He was the seventh American on the
5 moon.

At quarter past eleven on the same morning the Moon Rover was ready. Scott and Irwin started the Rover.

"Man, oh man!" cried Scott, "What a Grand Prix this is!"

The top speed was seven miles per hour.
10 Man's first drive on the moon was five miles long. The date was Saturday, July 31, 1971.

NASA

LISTEN & UNDERSTAND

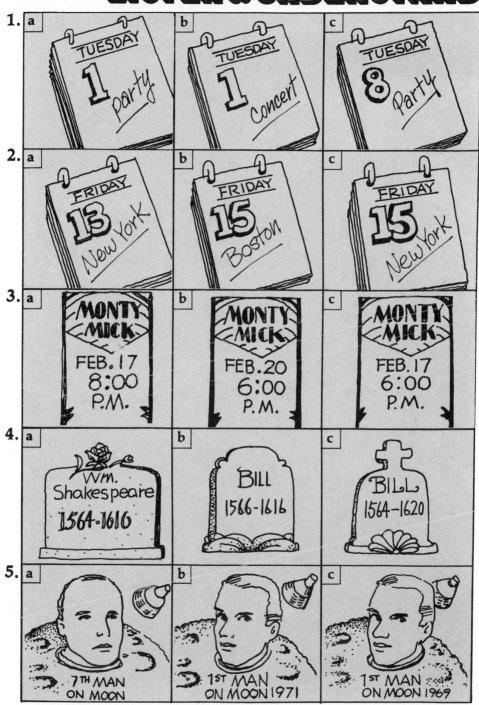

PRONUNCIATION

I.
play	hate	wait	radio
plate	cake	bake	face
today	game	eight	May
name	later	date	spaceship

My roommate is going to bake a cake later.

The date today is the eighth of May.

II.
type	fry	tire	fly
find	I	drive	tie
sign	dry	my	buy
five	white	nine	miles

I can't find my white tie.

My wife is going to drive five miles.

III.
now	house	towel	how
outside	hour	downtown	brown
blouse	out	our	announcing

The brown house is downtown.

How much are the blouses and towels?

IV. Now I'm going to write my name.

They can dry their faces on our towel.

I can play outside now.

We're going ninety-eight miles per hour!

I'm going to buy a brown raincoat, a white blouse
and a gray tie.

BASICS

USING NUMBERS:

DATES

5/10/41	May 10, 1941	the 10th of May, 1941
		the tenth of May, nineteen forty-one
		May tenth, nineteen forty-one
	1955	nineteen fifty-five
	1728	seventeen twenty-eight
	1872	eighteen seventy-two

USING PREPOSITIONS OF TIME:

IN	ON
in May	on Monday
in 1972	on May 10th
	on the 15th

AT	FOR
at 7 o'clock	for sixty years

VOCABULARY/EXPRESSIONS

announcing	had	top speed
birth	landed	wedding
born	last	weigh
calendar	miles per hour	
climbed out of	moon	Man, oh man!
date	ready	Sure.
die	record	Uh-oh.
drive	spaceship	

TEST YOURSELF

I. 1. Were you and George at the bank today?   No, ...

      2. Was Harry home last night?   No, ...

      3. Was Frank working yesterday?   Yes, ...

      4. Were your parents on vacation last week?   Yes, ...

II. 1. What was George doing when you arrived?

      2. What was Alice doing?

      3. What was Tom doing?

      4. What was Ann doing?

      5. What were they doing?

III. 1. Are they reading now?
      I think so. At least they... ... when I was there.

      2. Is he painting now?
      I think so. At least he... ... when I was there.

      3. Are they working now?
      I don't think so. At least they... ... when I was there.

      4. Is she jogging now?
      I don't think so. At least she... ... when I was there.

S	M	T	W	T	F	S
2 Mary – Tennis	3	4	5 Jack – New York	6	7	8

IV. 1. Monday is the ... day of the week.

    2. Tuesday is the ... day of the week.

    3. Friday is the ... day of the week.

    4. Saturday is the ... day of the week.

    5. What day was the third?   It was a ....

    6. When was Jack in New York?   On ... the ....

    7. When was Mary playing tennis?   On ... the....

V. 1. When was Beethoven born?   ... 1770.

    2. When did he die?   ... 1827.

    3. How long did he live?   ... 57 years.

VI. Dear Ernie,

    Thanks for your letter. Yes, I like Florida. I arrived ...
Saturday ... noon. I play tennis ... the morning. I swim
... the afternoon. Tonight I'm going to a movie ...
Mary Webber. Do you know her? There ... many girls
here. I want to come here ... 1983. I'm going to go
home ... the thirty-first. I'm going ... train. Can you
come to the station?

                  Your friend,

                  Alex

UNIT 10 TEN

SURE...

—Dad, please help me
with my homework.
—Sure, son. What do
you want to know?

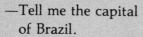

—Tell me the capital
of Brazil.
—Hmmm. I don't know.

—What's to the south
of Mexico?
—I don't know that either.

—Well, which state is
north of California?
—Ahh...er.... Isn't your
mother calling you?

EXERCISE CLASS

1. Put your feet together.
   Jump up and down ten times.

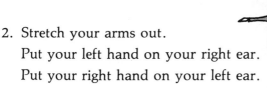

2. Stretch your arms out.
   Put your left hand on your right ear.
   Put your right hand on your left ear.
   Do this twenty times.

3. Put your hands on the top of your head.
   Put your head far back.
   Put your hands on the back of your neck.
   Put your head far forward.
   Do this ten times.

4. Touch your left foot with the fingers of your right hand.
   Touch your right foot with the fingers of your left hand.
   Do this twelve times.

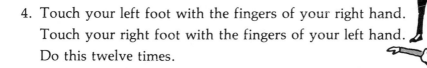

5. Lie on the floor.
   Bend your knees.
   Touch your knees with your forehead.
   Do this three times.

6. Lie on the floor.
   Lift your legs five times.

7. Stand up.
   Jump up and down fifteen times.
   Now you are fit—or dead!

—Here. **Take this cough medicine.**
—What kind is it?
—It's the best kind of **cough medicine. Take** it!
—Okay, okay. I'm **taking** it!

1. **Buy this perfume.**
2. **Play this music.**
3. **Use this paint.**
4. **Order this typewriter.**

5. **Watch this trick.**
6. **Read this love story.**
7. **Eat this cake.**
8. **Drink this tea.**

What is the capital of England?   **London is.**

1. What is the capital of Australia?   Canberra is.
2. What is the capital of Canada?   Ottawa is.
3. What is the capital of Argentina?   Buenos Aires is.
4. What is the capital of Colombia?   Bogotá is.
5. What is the capital of the U.S.A.?   Washington, D.C. is.

What can you say about London?   **London is the capital of England.**

1. What can you say about Moscow?   Moscow is the capital of Russia.

2. What can you say about Tokyo?   Tokyo is the capital of Japan.

3. What can you say about Mexico City?   Mexico City is the capital of Mexico.

4. What can you say about Brasília?   Brasília is the capital of Brazil.

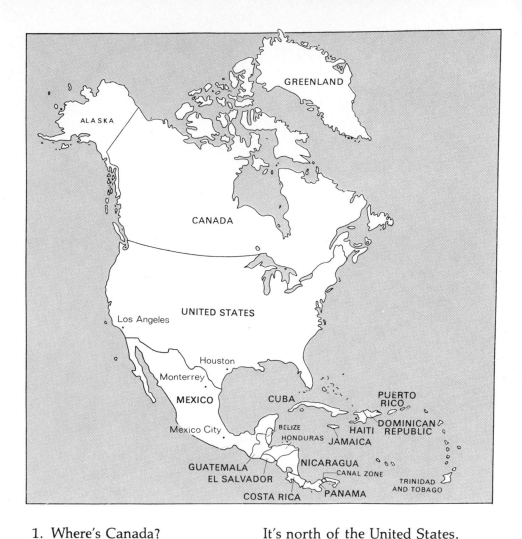

1. Where's Canada?   It's north of the United States.
2. Where's Mexico?   It's south of the United States.
3. Where's Puerto Rico?   It's east of the Dominican Republic.
4. Where's Guatemala?   It's west of Honduras.
5. Is Monterrey to the north
   or to the south of Mexico City? It's to the north.
6. Is Los Angeles to the east
   or to the west of Houston?   It's to the west.

ON YOUR OWN

Now ask and answer questions with a friend.

One day Mr. Grump and Mr. Bold were talking on a bus.

MR. GRUMP: I remember the summer of 1963. It rained from May to September.

MR. BOLD: You're wrong. *I* remember the summer of 1963. It didn't rain for three months.

MR. GRUMP: You have a very bad memory! There were no apples in my garden because of the rain.

MR. BOLD: No apples! I picked thousands of apples! It was very hot and sunny.

MR. GRUMP: I'm going to be angry in a minute. It poured all the time. I know I'm right.

MR. BOLD: Listen, Grump.

MR. GRUMP: No, *you* listen, Bold....

There was a student sitting behind them. She was listening to them.

MISS PITTS: Excuse me, but you are both wrong. I remember the summer of 1963. It started raining on May 10th and stopped on July 13th. It was hot and sunny every day from the 14th of July to the 29th of August. I think that takes care of this argument. Bye.

MR. GRUMP: Hurump! These students of today! They think they know everything.

MR. BOLD: Yes. I never did that kind of thing when I was their age. And of course, she was wrong.

MR. GRUMP: Of course. *I* was right.

MR. BOLD: You were NOT right, Grump. *I* was right!

MR. GRUMP: Now, wait a minute....

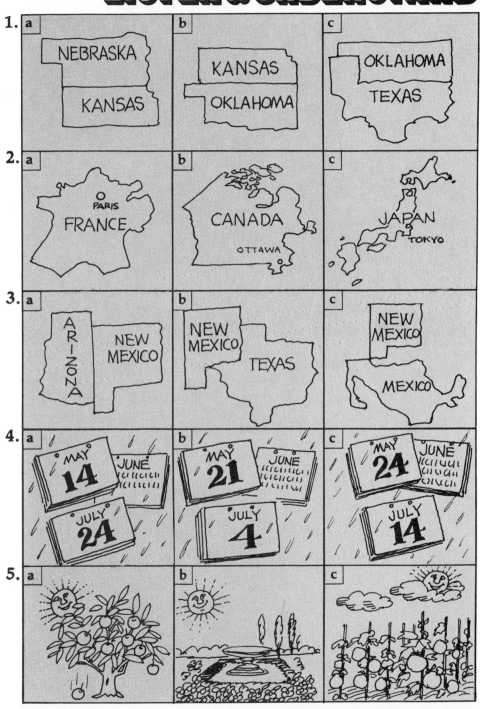

BASICS

IMPERATIVES: **Tell** me the capital of Brazil.
Stand up.
Watch this trick.

DIRECTIONS:

	the **north**	
to	the **south**	of
	the **east**	
	the **west**	

GENITIVE OF: the capital **of** Brazil

VOCABULARY/EXPRESSIONS

argument	left	stopped
because of	lie	stretch
bend	love story	take medicine
best	memory	takes care of
capital	minute	thing
cough medicine	neck	thousands
dead	north	times
east	order	together
exercise class	perfume	the top of
fit	put	touch
forehead	remember	trick
forward	right	typewriter
garden	south	west
jump	stand up	What kind...?
kind	state	

—Whose driver's license is that?
—I bet you can't guess. Look at the photo.
—Let me see. It's Tom's!
—Right. The photo doesn't look like him, does it?
—No, but my photo doesn't look like *me*, either.

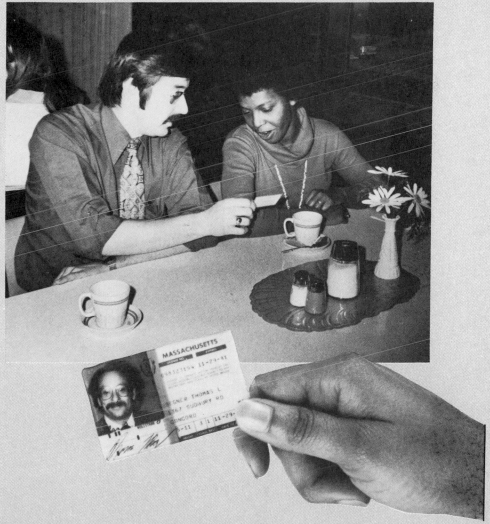

Tom	Maria	the teacher	Mr. Brown
motorcycle	bike	car	boat
radio	record player	typewriter	tape recorder
dogs	parrots	cats	horses
clothes	books	shoes	records

1. Whose motorcycle is it?   It's Tom's

2. Whose bike is it?   It's Maria's.

3. Whose car is it?   It's the teacher's.

4. Whose boat is it?   It's Mr. Brown's.

5. Whose dogs are they?   They're Tom's.

6. Whose radio is it?

7. Whose tape recorder is it?

8. Whose typewriter is it?

9. Whose record player is it?

10. Whose parrots are they?

11. Whose cats are they?

12. Whose horses are they?

13. Whose clothes are they?

14. Whose books are they?

15. Whose shoes are they?

16. Whose records are they?

1. —Does Maria have a motorcycle?
   —No, she doesn't.
   —Well, whose motorcycle *is* it?
   —It's Tom's.

2. —Does Tom have horses?
   —No, he doesn't.
   —Well, whose horses *are* they?
   —They're Mr. Brown's.

3. —Does the teacher have a record player?
   —No, she doesn't.
   —Well, whose record player *is* it?
   —It's Maria's.

4. —Does Mr. Brown have cats?
   —No, he doesn't.
   —Well, whose cats *are* they?
   —They're the teacher's.

5. —Does Mr. Brown have a radio?
   —No, he doesn't.
   —Whose radio *is* it?
   —It's Tom's.

—Whose **horses** are those?
—Which ones?
—The **brown** ones.
—Oh, they're the **farmer's**.

1.  white

2.  old

3.  American

4.  new

5.  orange

6. black and white

THE V.I.P. *(very important person)*

The plane was waiting at gate 34. The newspaper photographers were waiting with their cameras. They were tired. It was 11:30 at night. In the First Class Lounge, the newspaper reporters were waiting too.

—Hi, Frank. Where is the "big man?"
—I don't know.
—When does his plane leave?
—It takes off in twenty minutes.

The President of the country and his secretary were waiting.
—What time is it, Jane?
—Twenty minutes to twelve, sir.
—Where is he?
—I don't know, sir.
—What does he look like?
—Well, sir, he's....

Two policemen were standing at the door.
—He's late, isn't he?
—Yeah. I hope he comes soon, don't you?
—Yes. I'm tired. I want to go home.

The President walked to the microphone.
—Ladies and gentlemen, I am sorry, but Professor Santo isn't here. As you know, Professor Santo is the winner of the Nobel Peace Prize. He is going to Stockholm, the capital of Sweden, to accept the prize from the King. At least, he *was* going to Sweden.

"SAS announces the departure of its flight 279 to Stockholm, gate 34. All aboard, please."

—Wow! That's his flight! They're not going to wait for him.
—That's a good story... the Professor missed the plane!

The flight attendants closed the door. Then one of them jumped in surprise. A man was coming out of the lavatory. Was he a hijacker? No, it was Professor Santo!

—I hate publicity. Where's my seat?

LISTEN & UNDERSTAND

BASICS

DETERMINERS:

Whose motorcycle is it?   It's the woman's.

Whose horses are they?   They're Janet's.

Which ones?   The brown ones.

VOCABULARY/EXPRESSIONS

accept	record player
announces	seat
bet	surprise
bike	tape recorder
boat	takes off
departure	winner
gentlemen	
hijacker	All aboard.
lavatory	as you know….
look like	Let me see.
parrots	Wow!
photo	Yeah.
prize	
publicity	

UNIT 12
TWELVE

—Daddy, what's a grizzly bear?
—A grizzly bear is an animal that lives in a forest.

—Daddy, what's a forest?
—A forest is a place where wild animals live.

—Daddy, what's a wild animal?
—A wild animal is an animal that hunters hunt.

—Daddy, what's a hunter?
—A hunter is a person who hunts wild animals...
like grizzly bears.

—But Daddy! What *is* a grizzly bear?
—Oh, I give up!

Flowers grow in a garden.
A garden is a place where flowers grow.

1. People work in a factory.

2. Students learn at school.

3. Horses run at a race track.

4. A train stops at a station.

5. People buy things in a store.

6. Many trees grow in a forest.

7. Secretaries work in an office.

A **disco** is a place where people **dance.**

1. school

2. library

3. bookstore

4. beach

5. restaurant

6. bar

7. bank

8. park

A taxi driver drives a taxi.

A taxi driver is a person who drives a taxi.

1. A photographer takes pictures.

2. A nurse works in a hospital.

3. An author writes books.

4. A reporter writes for a newspaper.

5. A gardener takes care of a garden.

6. A pilot flies a plane.

7. A librarian works in a library.

A taxi driver is a person who **drives a taxi.**

1. A teacher

2. A secretary

3. An artist

4. A storekeeper

5. A salesman

6. An author

7. A waiter

8. A mother

I go to work by bus. I usually catch the same bus every morning - the 8:15. I usually see the same people every morning, too.

First I get on the bus. I say "Good morning, Frank." Frank
5   is the man who drives the bus. Sometimes he says "Good morning." Sometimes he doesn't!

Then I look for a good seat. I like a place where I can see out the window. Mrs. Sanchez always sits in the first seat. She gets on the bus at the bus station. She gets off at the
10   corner where the hospital is. She's a nurse at the hospital.

Mr. Rank, the man who works at the bank, always sits in the second seat. Anita Gray, a girl who teaches an exercise class on TV, usually sits behind Mr. Rank. I say "Good morning" to them and walk to the third seat.

15   The bus goes along Green St. It passes a big factory where they make automobile parts. A lot of people who work at the factory get on the bus. They are the men and women who work at night. Then the bus turns left and crosses Main St. In about five minutes the bus comes to my stop. I
20   get off at the corner where the park begins. There's a big office building across the street. That's the building where I work.

LISTEN & UNDERSTAND

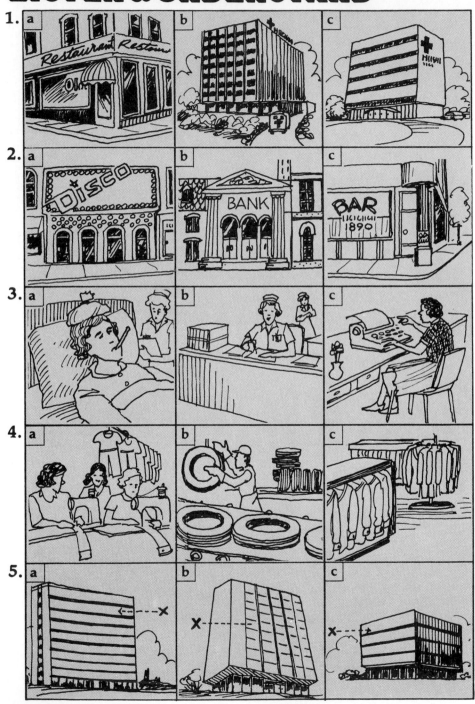

PRONUNCIATION

I.   guit_ar_   _ar_m   sc_ar_f

      f_ar_   _ar_my   y_ar_d

      _ar_e   b_ar_   h_ar_d

The army officer had a scarf on his arm.

The bar is not far from here.

II.   d_ear_   _ear_   engin_ee_r

      h_ere_   y_ear_   h_ear_s

The engineer is here, dear.

He hears with one ear.

III.   _ai_rport   h_ai_r   th_ei_r

      ch_ai_r   p_ea_r   th_ere_

      b_ea_r   squ_are_   we_ar_

What are you going to wear to the airport?

Give the bear a pear.

IV.   There are some bars on the square.

They are here every year.

The bear hears the guitar.

The army is very hard.

His ears, arms and hair look good.

BASICS

ADJECTIVE CLAUSES:

A grizzly bear is an animal **that lives in a forest.**

A forest is a place **where wild animals live.**

A hunter is a person **who hunts wild animals.**

VOCABULARY/EXPRESSIONS

across	forest	person
along	gardener	place
animal(s)	get(s) off	race track
artist	get(s) on	reporter
author	grizzly bear	restaurant
automobile parts	grow	salesman
bar	hospital	secretaries
beach	hunter	storekeeper
begins	hunts	wild
bookstore	learn	
building	librarian	I give up!
corner	look for	
crosses	out	
factory	park	
flowers	passes	

TEST YOURSELF

I.

1. What's the capital of England? ... is.

2. What can you say about Tokyo? Tokyo is ....

3. What can you say about Brasília?

4. What can you say about Ottawa?

5. Canada is...of the United States.

6. Is Mexico to the north of the United States? No, it's....

7. Is Puerto Rico to the west of Mexico? No, it's....

II.

Bill	Anita	the boy	the girl	the man
motorcycle	record player	piano	typewriter	cats
radio	records	horse	flowers	boots
soccer ball	gloves	backgammon game	tennis court	boat

1. Whose motorcycle is it?

2. Whose typewriter is it?

3. Whose cats are they?

4. Whose records are they?

5. Does Bill have a horse? No, he...
   Well, whose horse *is* it? ....

6. Does Anita have a radio? ....
   Well, whose radio *is* it? ....

III. People work in a factory.

A factory is a place where people work.

Write sentences in the same way for these:

1.

2.

3.

4.

5.

IV. A taxi driver drives a taxi.

A taxi driver is a person who drives a taxi.

Write sentences in the same way for these:

1.

2.

3.

4.

5.

GRAMMAR HIGHLIGHTS

THE SIMPLE PRESENT (Unit 1)

STATEMENTS:	I want to play tennis. They have a guitar.
YES-NO QUESTIONS:	Do you want to play football? Do you have a racket? Do you like to dance? Do you like apples?
INFORMATION QUESTIONS:	What do you want to do? When do you want to play? What do you have in there? How do you come to school?
SHORT ANSWERS:	Yes, I do. No, I don't.

THE SIMPLE PRESENT—THIRD PERSON SINGULAR
(Units 2, 3 and 4)

STATEMENT:	Tom likes sports cars, but he doesn't like motorcycles.
YES-NO QUESTION:	Does s(he) play tennis?
INFORMATION QUESTION:	What does s(he) do for a living?
SHORT ANSWERS:	Yes, s(he) does. No, s(he) doesn't.
THIRD-PERSON -S FORM:	He gets dressed in the morning. She eats breakfast. It sleeps all afternoon.
NEGATIVE QUESTION FORMS:	Don't you ever go to parties? Doesn't he always make the beds? Ann usually comes on time, doesn't she?
THIRD PERSON -ES FORM:	brush brushes teach teaches dress dresses watch watches
Y/IES FORMS:	carry carries fly flies dry dries hurry hurries empty empties try to tries to

THIRD-PERSON [-S], [-Z] AND [-IZ] FORMS:

[-S]		[-Z]		[-IZ]	
cook	cooks	arrive	arrives	brush	brushes
cost	costs	clean	cleans	change	changes
drink	drinks	comb	combs	chase	chases
eat	eats	come	comes	crash	crashes
get up	gets up	deliver	delivers	dance	dances
help	helps	drive	drives	dress	dresses
lift	lifts	find	finds	kiss	kisses
like	likes	leave	leaves	miss	misses
make	makes	open	opens	push	pushes
put on	puts on	play	plays	teach	teaches
sleep	sleeps	run	runs	wash	washes
speak	speaks	see	sees	watch	watches
take off	takes off	shave	shaves		
talk	talks				
wait	waits				
walk	walks				
work	works				
write	writes				

THE SIMPLE PAST TENSE (Unit 7)

STATEMENTS: Anna cleaned my room.
                     They didn't have any candles.

INFORMATION QUESTION: When did they arrive?

[-d]		[-t]	
arrive	arrived	bake	baked
call	called	brush	brushed
change	changed	cook	cooked
clean	cleaned	dress	dressed
close	closed	kiss	kissed
deliver	delivered	look	looked
iron	ironed	miss	missed
open	opened	park	parked
play	played	pick up	picked up
return	returned	polish	polished
shorten	shortened	type	typed
travel	traveled	walk	walked
y → ied		wash	washed
carry	carried	watch	watched
copy	copied	wax	waxed
dry	dried	**[-id]**	
empty	emptied	hate	hated
fry	fried	paint	painted
hurry	hurried	plant	planted
marry	married	point	pointed
try	tried	rent	rented
worry	worried	wait	waited
		want	wanted

PRESENT PROGRESSIVE FUTURE FORM: *GOING TO*
(Unit 5)

GO + NOUN/GO + VERB:

He	is		England.
She			
		going to	Mexico.
We			
You	are		Canada.
They			
He	is		study.
She			
		going to	read.
We			
You	are		work.
They			

Where is he going? → He is going to England.
What is he going to do?→ He is going to study.

THE SIMPLE PRESENT AND PRESENT PROGRESSIVE
(Unit 2)

General	**Limited**
(Characteristic, habitual)	*(Temporary)*
What does he do?	What is he doing now?
He cooks.	He's eating.

USES OF THE PRESENT TENSES (Unit 5)

Time	Tense
He **brushes** his teeth (every day).	Simple Present
He **is brushing** his teeth (now).	Present Progressive
He **is going to brush** his teeth (tomorrow).	Present Progressive (future)
She **is going** to England (next summer).	Present Progressive (future)

THE SIMPLE PAST AND PAST PROGRESSIVE (Unit 8)

Simple Past: (completed action)

What did you do?   I danced.

Past Progressive: (during the past)
What were you doing?   I was dancing.
What were they doing when you arrived? They were dancing.
She wasn't working when I was there.
They weren't reading when I was there.

HAVE (TO EAT/DRINK) (Unit 3)

I usually have coffee for breakfast.

TO BE (Unit 8)

	Present	Past
I	am	was
He/She/It	is	was
You/We/They	are	were

THERE + TO BE (Unit 8)

Present there is / there are   **Past** there was / there were

LIKE, WANT + INFINITIVE (Unit 1)

Do you like to dance?   Yes, I do. / No, I don't.

What do you want to wear?   I want to wear jeans.

AUXILIARIES: DO/DID (Units 1, 2, 6)

Do	I you we they drink milk?	Yes,	I you we they **do.**	No,	I you we they **don't.**
Does	he she it drink milk?	Yes,	he she it **does.**	No,	he she it **doesn't.**
Did	I you we they he she it drink milk?	Yes,	I you we they he she it **did.**	No,	I you we they he she it **didn't.**

IMPERATIVES (Unit 10)

Tell me the capital of Brazil.

ADJECTIVE (RELATIVE) CLAUSES (Unit 12)

A grizzly bear is an animal **that lives in a forest**.
A forest is a place **where wild animals live**.
A hunter is a person **who hunts wild animals**.

ADVERBS OF FREQUENCY (Unit 3)

frequently
often   **seldom**
He **always**   gets up early. She **almost never** works hard.
sometimes   **never**
usually

PREPOSITIONS OF TIME (Unit 9)

in May   **on** Monday   **at** 7 o'clock
in 1972   **on** May 10th   **for** sixty years
                on the 15th

GENITIVE: *OF* (Unit 10)

the capital **of** Brazil

CONTRACTIONS (Units 1, 2, 6, 8)

let us → let's   was not → wasn't
does not → doesn't   were not → weren't
did not → didn't

ORDINAL NUMBERS AND DATES (Unit 9)

1 first	7 seventh	13 thirteenth
2 second	8 eighth	14 fourteenth
3 third	9 ninth	15 fifteenth
4 fourth	10 tenth	20 twentieth
5 fifth	11 eleventh	21 twenty-first
6 sixth	12 twelfth	30 thirtieth

May 10, 1941   the 10th of May, 1941
    or   the tenth of May, nineteen forty-one
  5/10/41   May tenth, nineteen forty-one

        1955   nineteen fifty-five
        1728   seventeen twenty-eight
        1872   eighteen seventy-two

REVIEW HIGHLIGHTS

POSSESSIVE ADJECTIVES

This is **my / your / his / her** friend.

Our / Your / Their dog is very big.

NOUNS

Plurals

Regular: bank orange bus country church
banks oranges buses countries churches

Irregular: child man woman foot tooth
children men women feet teeth

PREPOSITIONS OF PLACE

The tie is **on / under** the chair.   Don is **at** the bus stop.

Mr. Jones is **in front of / behind** Mrs. Rivera.   Lucy is **in** the bedroom.

PRONOUNS

SUBJECT		OBJECT	
I	he we	me	him us
you	she you	you	her you
	it they		it them

VERBS

SIMPLE PRESENT **to be** (Units 1, 2, 6)

I **am** Elena Silva.
You **are** a nurse.
He/She **is** an accountant.
It **is** cold.

We / You / They **are** happy.

PRESENT PROGRESSIVE

I **am going** to the supermarket.
You **are buying** bread.
He **is drinking** coffee.
She **is reading** a book.
It **is raining**.

We **are sitting** in the kitchen.

You **are watching** television.

They **are dancing.**

WORD LIST

about (approx.) 47
accept 107
alarm clock 35
All Aboard. 107
almost 22
alone 78
along 115
always 21
ambulance 59
animal(s) 110
announces 107
announcing 89
answers (v.) 57
any 68
apartment 67
argument 100
arrive(s) 25
arrived 64
artist 114
as (you know) 107
ask 25
asks 57
asleep 46
at least 82
author 113
automobile parts 115

back (yard) 68
backgammon board 3
bag 36
baggage 12
bake(d) 68
ball 3
bar 112
bathing suit 46
beach 112
because 23
beef 2
begins 115
bend 97
best 98
bet (v.) 103
bicycle 6
bike 104
birth 89
birthday 68
boat 104
born 88
box (n.) 64
brushed 66
brushes (v.) 24
burned 70

buy 8
by 1

cake 54
calendar 87
call (v.) 57
called 64
calling 96
candles 68
capital 96
carried 65
carries 35
carry 12
catch 36
changed 64
changes (v.) 32
chase 34
chases 32
chicken 2
chickens 66
cigarette 23
cleaned 63
cleaning 15
cleans 33
climbed out of 90
close(s) 57
closed 64
coconuts 2
comb(s) 24
come on 31
comes 22
comes out of 36
cook (v.) 12
cooked 66
cooks 13
cookbook 46
copied 65
copy 65
corner 115
cost(s) (v.) 25
cough medicine 98
crash(es) 35
cried 90
cries 36
crosses (v.) 115

dancer 32
dances (v.) 32
date (n.) 90
date (v.) 87
dead 97
deliver(ed) 64

delivers 13
departure 107
did (aux.) 53
did (main) 100
die 88
diet 21
directly 25
dirty 39
disco 6
dishes 35
do for a living 15
does 11
door 57
doors 53
down 97
downtown 1
dress (v.) 34
dresses (v.) 36
dried 65
drink (v.) 5
drinks (v.) 34
drive (n.) 90
drives (v.) 13
dry (-ies) 35

east 99
eat 5
eats 22
eighteenth 86
eighth 86
either 2
eleventh 86
emptied 65
empty (adj.) 68
empty (-ies) 35
ever 23
everything 25
exercise class 97

face 24
factory 111
fifteenth 86
fifth 86
finally 68
find(s) 33
fingers 97
first (adj.) 90
first (n.) 85
fit (adj.) 97
flowers 111
fly (-ies) (v.) 35
forehead 97

ANSWERS TO THE *TEST YOURSELF* SECTIONS

Pp. 29-30
I. 1. (a) 2. (b) 3. (c) 4. (a) 5. (b) 6. (b) 7. (b) 8. (c) 9. (a)
II. 1. she's dancing 2. she's playing (table tennis) 3. he's cooking 4. he's singing 5. He's a chef. He's eating. 6. She's a rider. She's cleaning her boots.
III. 1. to go to the movies. 2. by bus. 3. in the morning. 4. I want to have lunch at noon. 5. usually go to sleep at midnight.

Pp. 51-52
I. rings, walks, washes, dresses, uniform, hurries, carries, changes, plays, watches
II. 1. cleans 2. carries 3. pushes 4. puts on 5. writes 6. flies 7. chases
III. 1. are doing 2. watches 3. is going to wash 4. is going to/is going to 5. Where is 6. When is 7. going IV. 1. is she going 2. does the alarm clock ring 3. playing football 4. going to watch TV. 5. going to listen to the radio 6. Where is she going 7. It's

Pp. 75-76
I. 1. (b) 2. (b) 3. (c) 4. (c) 5. (b) 6. (c) 7. (a) 8. (b) 9. (a)
II. 1. to 2. did 3. didn't 4. don't 5. doesn't 6. Did 7. opened 8. shortened 9. dried 10. When did you arrive 11. What did he do/What did he park 12. What did she do/Who did she kiss 13. ironed 14. emptied 15. typed 16. wanted...cake 17. waxed...car 18. planted...tree 19. watched TV 20. carried...box.

Pp. 94-95
I. 1. we weren't 2. he wasn't 3. he was 4. they were II. 1. He was playing the guitar. 2. She was drying her hair. 3. He was washing the dishes. 4. She was ironing. 5. They were jogging. III. 1. were reading 2. was painting 3. weren't working 4. wasn't jogging IV. 1. second 2. third 3. sixth 4. seventh 5. Monday 6. Wednesday/fifth 7. Sunday/second V. 1. In 2. In 3. For VI. on, at, in, in, with, are, in, on, by

Pp. 119-120-121
I. 1. London 2. the capital of Japan. 3. It's the capital of Brazil. 4. It's the capital of Canada. 5. to the north 6. to the south of the United States. 7. to the east of Mexico. II. 1. It's Bill's. 2. It's the girl's.   3. They're the man's. 4. They're Anita's. 5. doesn't./It's the boy's.   6. No, she doesn't./It's Bill's. III. 1. Flowers grow in a garden. A garden is a place where flowers grow. 2. Students learn at school. (A) school is a place where students learn. 3. Trees grow in a forest. A forest is a place where trees grow. 4. Secretaries work in an office. An office is a place where secretaries work. 5. Horses run at a race track. A race track is a place where horses run. IV. 1. A nurse works in a hospital. A nurse is a person who works in a hospital. 2. A pilot flies a plane. A pilot is a person who flies a plane. 3. A reporter writes for a newspaper. A reporter is a person who writes for a newspaper. 4. A photographer takes pictures. A photographer is a person who takes pictures. 5. A librarian works in a library. A librarian is a person who works in a library.

INDEX

Grammar

Adjectives
  adjective (relative) clauses: *that,*
    where, who, 110–115
  possessive (R), 31, 32, 39
Adverbs
  adverbial clause: *when,* 81, 82
  of frequency, 20–24
  of time and place, 42
Contractions
  didn't, 56–60
  doesn't, 11, 12, 16, 17
  it's, they're (R), 103–106
  let's, 3
  wasn't, weren't, 78, 80 ,82
Nouns
  count and mass (R), 2
  singular possessives: *'s* (R), 55,
    103–106
Possessives
  adjectives (R), 31, 32, 39
  genitive: *of,* 96–98, 100
  singular nouns (R), 55,
    103–106
Prepositions
  by + transportation (R), 6
  time phrases:
    at (night) (R), 7, 89
    for (52 years), 88, 89
    in (1943), 88, 90
    in the (morning) (R), 7
    on (Tuesday, May 5), 87, 89
Pronouns
  he, she, it (R), 11–15
  I, you, we, they (R), 1–8
Question words
  how, what, where, when, why (R), 1,
    4–8, 43–46
  who (R), 65, 66
  whose, which (R), 103–106

Verbs
  auxiliaries
    did, didn't, 53, 56–60
    do, don't, 2–8, 15, 54, 55, 60
    does, doesn't, 11–17, 55, 60
    have (meaning to eat or drink),
      21, 22
  imperatives, 96–98
  like, want + infinitives, 1–3, 5–7
  past progressive, 77, 79, 81, 82
  present progressive (R), 15, 45
  present progressive future
    form: *going to*
    going to + verb, 42, 44–47, 87
    going to + place noun, 43, 46
  simple past, 53, 56–60
    final $/-d/$, $/-t/$, $/-id/$ sounds,
      63–70
    -y to *-ied* forms, 65
    was, were, weren't, 78–80, 86
  simple present, 2–4, 6, 8, 20–25
    am/is/are (R), 44
    negative questions: *don't,*
      doesn't, 22, 23
    third person singular
      final $/-s/$, $/-z/$ sounds,
        11–17, 22–25
      final *-es* spelling, 32
      final $/-s/$, $/-z/$, $/-iz/$ sounds,
        31–39, 110, 113–115
      -y to *-ies* spelling, 35
  there is/are, there was/wasn't, 80

(R) = (Review)

Listening Comprehension

9, 18, 26, 40, 48, 61, 68, 83, 101,
108

Reading Comprehension

8, 16, 17, 24, 25, 36, 47, 57, 68, 79,
80, 97, 100, 107

Pronunciation

Functions

Vocabulary